For Nevaeh & Maya, who taught me to see the world in color.

A Note from the Author

Since this original work first released via an email series in 2018, my learning has continued and vastly deepened. One of the risks I take as a writer putting myself out there is that I allow people to see me right where I am. Sometimes they see me and are able to see themselves more clearly. Other times I hear that I've given them language they never had before. Occasionally, but not often, readers shake their head in disapproval. However you see me, I hope you know I'm doing my very best. Though it's true there will always be moments down the road of enlightenment, I believe it's a disservice to withhold what we have today. This work isn't perfect, but I'm proud of it. I believe God called me to write it so that women all around the world could experience transformation. However, I feel it is worth acknowledging that space is a luxury. Fighting for and creating space in your life comes from a place of privilege; one many people do not have. There are people I love dearly in my corner of the world who live day to day in survival mode. They may never have the opportunity to plan for the future, begin creative pursuits purely for enjoyment, or afford a mental health day off work. I don't share this to make you feel bad, but if you feel a little bit uncomfortable that's alright. Chances are, we're a lot alike. I simply want to acknowledge that this devotional is written from a place of privilege and is not realistically applicable for all. My hope and prayer is that this devotional lands in the hands of women who learn how to create space and use it well. Space used well is not selfish. Space used well ultimately leads to privilege spent well. We may not always get it right, but may we never stay stagnant in fear of getting it wrong.

We are more than our doing. We need rest. Life's too short not to enjoy it.

Introduction

I was on a run when it hit me; a spark of joy
and a bit of anxiety all at once. My birthday
was right around the corner and deep
reflection began as it always does.

*How would I spend the next year? What could
I do to honor myself? Would I let another
month go by wishing my life was more of this
and a little less of that or would I do
something to create change?*

I declared in the midst of a sweaty mile that I
was not going to let another year go by
where I remained the same. One foot in
front of the other, I started moving at a
faster pace. I envisioned looking at myself in
the mirror.

*Who am I? Do I like me? What needs to
change?*

Surprisingly, the answers weren't far behind.

*I am a wife, daughter, mother, friend, believer,
fighter, doer, advocate. I am always in a
hurry, always too busy for people and the*

things I genuinely enjoy spending my time on. I am exhausted, depleted, and angry. I am tired; so very tired.

Salty tears and sweat drops streamed down my face.

Who am I? I am good. I am created in the image of God, therefore inside of me is the innate goodness of God.

Do I like me? Not really.

With that, I came to a halt.

I can't keep living this way. To hell with the hustle. I need rest. I want to play. I'm done working my life away.

The decision was made and I prayed to God.

Help me to have a year of space. God, please let it be one of learning how to say no instead of filling my calendar with obligations. Help me to invest in the things that matter, including myself.

Friend, my guess is that you have a similar longing or you wouldn't be reading this.

Everyday you pour out, but your cup is empty and there is nothing left to pour. You need to be replenished.

Let's make the next 30 days about refueling for the long haul. It's time to create healthy and sustainable rhythms of work, play and rest. We're going to do it by looking at the life of Jesus, digging into God's word, and getting practical.

My prayer is that you will not be the same person after you complete this journey.

Day 1
The Possibilities of a Life with Space

Love is patient, love is kind. It does not envy, it does not boast, it is not proud. It does not dishonor others, it is not self-seeking, it is not easily angered, it keeps no record of wrongs. Love does not delight in evil but rejoices with the truth. It always protects, always trusts, always hopes, always perseveres.

1 Corinthians 13:4-7

Years ago a pastor recommended I read through 1 Corinthians 13 replacing the word 'love' with my first name. He said to read it out loud, so I did:

"Manda is patient, Manda is kind. She does not envy, she does not boast, she is not proud. She does not dishonor others, she is not self-seeking, she is not easily angered, she keeps no record of wrongs. Manda does not delight in evil but rejoices with the truth. She always protects, always trusts, always hopes, always perseveres."

I remember the feeling — longing and shame tangled up in a single exhale. The words I spoke aloud were everything I ever wanted to be known for, but a far cry from reality. I desperately longed to be more patient and kind. The "not easily angered" part made me laugh a little. Could I, a hot-tempered, feisty woman, *ever* not be easily angered?

To have the people closest to me describe me the way love is described in this passage would mean some serious changes in my life. Little did I know the pathway to embodying love was simple: space. Space to be with Jesus.

Maybe you want to be a more loving and patient mom or perhaps you want to be available when the right person comes along? What if inside you is the most brilliant novel awaiting to be written or the next big invention awaiting to be known?

You need space; space to be with Jesus.

When we live beyond our limits, with a jam-packed schedule and an overwhelmed soul, our family and friends don't get our best.

We might be able to pull off a pleasant 60-second interaction at the grocery store, but what about the people closest to us? Do they get to be recipients of our love, kindness, patience, and gentleness?

For me, the answer is rarely. Not without adequate space.

When you read through the love passage replacing your name, what strikes you? What could a life with space produce in you?

Prayer

Lord, I know all I ever want ultimately boils down to a life that honors you. I know that when I spend time in your presence, I am changed; more loving, joyful, peace-filled, patient, kind, gentle, and self-controlled. I don't have to strive for the fruits of the spirit because they ooze out of me when I make time for you to work in me. Help me to see a

spacious life as one that glorifies you.
Forgive me for living without space. Amen.

Day 2
You Are in Charge of Your Space

"I have the right to do anything," you say—but not everything is beneficial. "I have the right to do anything" — but I will not be mastered by anything. 1 Corinthians 6:12

For so long, I said yes to everything. I let every text message, email, phone call, and invitation run my life. My schedule catered to accommodate everyone around me. It was exhausting.

One day, a dear family friend was hanging out at our home with my husband. He must have been paying attention as I frantically rushed around the house gathering my things while complaining aloud about the obligation I was headed for. Right as I was about to take off, he said something so matter of fact.

"Stop valuing other people's time more than yours. Your calendar is yours, not someone else's."

He caught my attention. Feeling a bit blindsided I asked, "And how do you suggest I do that?"

Thinking he wouldn't have any practical advice, he offered a few nuggets of wisdom.

"Whenever I receive a notification, I don't feel pressure or the need to reply right away. I don't go out when I really want to stay in. I don't say yes to anything I'm not interested in being a part of. You're the manager of your time and space, Manda! Stop letting other people run the show. Set boundaries. Start managing what you already own."

A light bulb went off as I closed the door behind me. *Duh*, I thought. I own my life and space. Why would I let friends, family, coworkers - especially people I don't even really like - manage it for me?

I'M IN CHARGE. Little ole' me!

When you try to fulfill other people's expectations or become who you think they want you to be, you end up losing who you are, losing your time and space, and most importantly: losing who God made you to be. You need to reclaim your space and start trusting God as if your life depends on Him. The secret is out... it does!

God continually reminds us that we can trust Him. He is ready to take our days, our time and space, and craft them into something beautiful. Something valuable. Something extraordinary. But first we have to give it over to Him. We have to take charge and stop letting everything and everyone else dictate our schedule.

Let go of empty excuses like "I'm busy" or "I don't know how to do that." It's liberating. Instead of playing the victim, drop the drama and own the fact that you are in charge of your life.

You don't have to go to that party.
You don't have to work beyond the hours you are paid.
You don't have to volunteer for everything that comes up at your church.
You don't have to keep your kitchen sink empty at all times.

You don't have to have allow notifications on your phone.

You don't *have* to do anything. Because you are in charge of your space.

Are you going to continue letting others run the show or will you reclaim what's already yours and start trusting God to make something beautiful out of it?

Prayer

Jesus, how much better and sweeter life is when I am reminded of who I am and who I belong to. Thank you for being patient with me. Thanks for tugging on my heart to help me see I wasn't meant for a life that's out of control busy, dictated by others and unenjoyable. I'm sorry for the ways I've allowed everything and everyone else to have more power over my time and schedule than you. You have authority over my life. Help me to use my free will to honor you and delight in the everyday. Amen.

Day 3
If You Don't Control Your Space, Who Will?

Do not run until your feet are bare and your throat is dry. But you said, 'It's no use! I love foreign gods, and I must go after them.'
Jeremiah 2:25

When I got my driver's license, I'm pretty sure the first place I ventured off to solo was the tanning salon. (A decade later, I could kick myself!) I remember my mom standing in the driveway as I slowly backed out. "Manda Sue, don't ever let your gas tank get too empty. The minute you hit half tank, get to the nearest gas station and fill all the way up." she sternly instructed.

My mom wasn't just nagging to nag. She didn't want me to run out of gas and she also knew that running on empty could negatively affect my car's performance and create unnecessary anxiety in me.

Turns out, this applies to more than just my car...

In my early twenties, I tried to run on empty. I didn't acknowledge my limitations. Sleep wasn't a priority. Saying "no" was unfamiliar. I ran myself ragged trying to be everything for everyone. I thought I was invincible. (Spoiler alert: I'm not.)

The result was anxiety and a less-than-ideal performance at my job and in my relationships. Like always, mom was right.

I don't want to always be counting down the days till my next vacation. I want to live in a rhythm of space that allows me to experience the joys of living.

This is hard work; shifting from a life that operates at 150% each day to a life that has a rhythm of space. Everyone wants a piece of us and there just isn't enough to go around! As much as you may not want to admit it, you have a limited capacity. There is no way you can do it all. *Though we try, don't we?*

So, how do we reclaim what's ours? How do we make space?

Get back in the driver's seat and watch your gas gauge closely.

Space is what lies between rest and exhaustion. It's the difference between breathing freely and suffocating. We have to fight for it if we want to keep from running on empty. Unlike cars, we don't have a visual for when the tank requires more gas, but there are sure signs in life that serve as indicators of our need.

Pay attention to your mind, body, and spirit. I know I need more space when I become crabby for no reason, tired beyond belief, disinterested in things I love, easily offended and overwhelmed by non-issues.

Whether you are a fast-paced entrepreneur, college student, or stay-at-home mom, space has the potential to radically change your life and make it more sustainable. This isn't about becoming less productive or throwing in the towel. Space is like my mom's advice... a preventative measure to keep us going and eliminate unnecessary anxiety.

Prayer

God, forgive me for having idols. Forgive me for worshipping things and others by living my life in such a frantic hurry all the time. I long for a deep exhale with you. Will you fill my tank and help me to acknowledge when it is getting low? Teach me to pay attention to what my mind, body, and spirit are trying to tell me. I don't want to neglect my needs and ultimately my dependence upon you. I love you and I'm so thankful change is possible with you. Amen.

Day 4
Is a Life Without Space Really Living?

But Jesus often withdrew to lonely places and prayed. Luke 5:16

Confession: I really enjoy working at coffee shops because I love people watching and eavesdropping. Sometimes I have to fight the urge to intrude, especially when I overheard conversations like this one...

"I'm just going to do the best I can within the hours I have. I've worked too much and too hard... and for what?" her voice rising. "Where has it gotten me?!"

Her friend replied, reassuring her that all of her hard work had taken her so far! She pointed out her title and status, adding in a mention of the trip she recently took to Greece.

But the woman, with tears in her eyes, said, "I'm exhausted. I don't even know if any of it matters. I go home at night to an empty apartment. Yes, Greece was beautiful, but I didn't have anyone to share it with. I'm tired of rushing around and working late at the office, meanwhile everyone around me is out having a good time or spending the evening with someone they love. There's gotta be more."

Recognizing that life is too short and too precious to waste it on stressing and striving is the beginning of a beautiful surrender. It's the invitation for more joy, rest, and meaning. It's found in the margins; the in-between, hardly recognized space of our lives. Space that our society undervalues and even scoffs at. Space to breathe and face reality, to notice where we've lost ourselves... the place where Jesus meets us.

Without margin in my life, everything is a blur. It's no wonder I find myself complaining that I don't hear from God or I feel uncertain about a decision. I'm moving at the speed of light, going from one thing to the next, interacting with so many people, pouring out, only to plop down on the couch and pass out as soon as I'm home. Where's the time for my Lord and Savior?

Listen, you don't need a life coach or better friends. You need time! I hate to burst your bubble, but you and I have the same amount of time as everybody else. We need to make our time count; use it well. I'm talking about blocking out and protecting time just for space.

Space, by definition, is "a continuous area or expanse that is free, available, or unoccupied." We need time that is free, available, and unoccupied.

Even Jesus, the Son of God, (no big deal) needed space. And if He needed it, who am I to think I can live without it?

Say it with me. Decide for yourself. I want space and it is my job to create it.

Prayer

God, thank you for loving me even when I'm a frantic hot mess. Thanks for always inviting me in and waiting no matter how long I take. I'm sorry for the ways I've strived and hustled, doing life on my own. I'm sorry for missing out on what you have for me

because I'm too busy thinking what I have is more important. Humble me. Help me to realize I cannot do it all. And help me to realize I don't have to. I'm ready for space. Meet me in the margins, Jesus.
Amen.

Day 5
Is Space Worth Fighting For?

Are you tired? Worn out? Burned out on religion? Come to me. Get away with me and you'll recover your life. I'll show you how to take a real rest. Walk with me and work with me—watch how I do it. Learn the unforced rhythms of grace. I won't lay anything heavy or ill-fitting on you. Keep company with me and you'll learn to live freely and lightly.
Matthew 11:28-30

"If only I had more time I'd

—————————————."

You'd what?

Workout. Volunteer. Meal prep. Read your Bible. Call your grandparents. Get to know your actual neighbors. Start tackling that project you've been dreaming of for years.

We weren't created to live this way—and we don't have to! Space really is worth fighting for. Jesus addressed this with his disciples in Matthew. He reminds us that getting away with him is how we recover. He shows us real rest by filling us up when we spend time in his presence. Don't you love the idea of living freely and lightly?

We're prone to tied up, heavy days. We wake up ready to maximize each moment before us... get ready as fast as possible, eat a quick breakfast (if you're lucky) before running out the door, fill every minute of the day with meetings, work, chores, driving, shopping, eating, emails, calls, social media, errands... *you get the idea.* Our days are full from the time we wake up until the time we crash in bed. Although we live very stuffed days, we often come to realize that we're quite unsatisfied because there's no time to do things we truly enjoy, let alone time to simply be still.

We need to BE with God. A church I used to work for stated it in our team values like this: **We need to be with God so that doing the work of God does not kill the work of God in us.**

We were created to be human beings, not human doings. We were meant to have space in our lives. Space for solitude, community, delight and wonder.

Brace yourself, though. You will have to fight yourself, society, cultural norms, other people — even people you are friends with — in order to have space. It will feel wonky at first. You will relapse occasionally and go to default busy-mode. Some may accuse you of being selfish.

But it's so worth it, friend. You, your family, friends, work, relationship with God and others are going to benefit as you fight for margin in your life.

I don't believe we need someone to tell us *how* to have space in our lives nearly as much as we need reminders that it is healthy and beautiful; worth the fight.

Fight for your space. Get away with God. You will live lighter, more freely, and you'll give others permission to do the same.

Prayer

Jesus, thank you for sharing the truth and offering freedom. I love spending time in your presence. Your word reminds me that I'm more than the sum of my accomplishments and am loved despite the ugliest parts of my heart. Please give me the confidence to fight for space in my life. You didn't create me to be a busy, overworked, unhappy human doing. Help me to fight for space to be with you. Amen

Day 6
Don't Let FOMO Keep You From a Spacious
Life

*I am the bread of life; whoever comes to me
shall not hunger, and whoever believes in me
shall never thirst.* John 6:35

Back in the pre-social media days, you could
miss the party or be without a significant
other and not lose any sleep over it. That's
no longer the case. People are literally losing
sleep over social media and the Fear Of
Missing Out.

When we feel like we are missing out
constantly, we take matters into our own
hands and we DO.

We do what we didn't feel like doing strictly
because we're afraid to miss out. We do
whatever we think will get us from point A to
point B the fastest. We do without ever
stopping to breathe because if we take a
break we might not get what we want. And
we keep on doing because a life without it, a
life with space, feels unproductive, scary,
slow, and risky...

Friend, this is a LIE and it's time to change the script. The problem isn't social media. The problem is our sin.

FOMO, and the root of our sinful nature, tells us over and over again that something other than Jesus will satisfy. It's just not true.

What Jesus declared to his disciples in John 6:35 is that we can only satisfy our spiritual hunger and sustain our spiritual life through a relationship with him. Just like bread (or in other words, nourishing food) must be eaten to sustain our life, Jesus must be invited into our daily walk to sustain spiritual life.

If the Fear Of Missing Out is keeping you from a life with space — room for your relationship with Jesus — you are in fear of missing out on the wrong thing! I propose you check your fear at the door and get to know Jesus instead.

Spend time in his word. Talk with him. You will receive a makes-no-sense peace. You will be reminded that no good thing is

withheld from you. You will see he is
working all things together for your good.
Live in light of his truths and proclaim them
to yourself.

Jesus is better than anything the world has
to offer. Only he can truly satisfy our desires.
A relationship with him is the only thing
worthy of FOMO.

Prayer

Jesus, I am hungry for you. I've been hungry
and tried to satisfy it on my own and it hasn't
worked out well. Help me to believe what
you said to your disciples and absorb it as
truth. Allow your words to change what I say
and do, even how I think. I'm sorry for
avoiding space in my life and neglecting time
with you while prioritizing and pursuing
other distractions. Thank you for loving me
regardless. I want to get rid of things that
trigger me to DO more and spend less time
with you. Help me to have the confidence to
walk in step with you daily so I'm not
tempted to buy the lie that I'm missing out
or falling behind or that anything else will
satisfy. Amen.

Day 7
The Cost of a Life Without Space

Then Jesus went to work on his disciples. "Anyone who intends to come with me has to let me lead. You're not in the driver's seat; I am. Don't run from suffering; embrace it. Follow me and I'll show you how. Self-help is no help at all. Self-sacrifice is the way, my way, to finding yourself, your true self. What kind of deal is it to get everything you want but lose yourself? What could you ever trade your soul for?" Matthew 16:24-26

When we look at the life of Jesus, there's one word that can be used to describe him that rubs me the wrong way: relaxed. However, it's undeniable as I read through the gospels. Jesus was, in fact, relaxed.

I've never liked that word because it is often associated with lazy, slow or inefficient. Yet, Jesus was relaxed and accomplished a great deal! I'm wonderstruck by the rhythm of his life.

Jesus wasn't rushed or reactive. He never seemed bothered by interruptions or distractions. He wasn't a workaholic. He often spent time alone in prayer for hours. His pace is a far cry from my frantic, hurried life. My usual response to "How are you?" being "busy" and my frivolous spending are not evidence of a life that follows him.

I struggle with being late constantly and valuing progress and productivity over people. But Jesus, he never chooses anything over people.

A life without space isn't relaxed or easeful. It doesn't look like the way of Jesus.

When we operate at or near 100% capacity, we have no time for interruptions. No opportunities to see God outside of our to-do lists and jam-packed schedules. Yet, I would argue this is primarily where God is found: in the space and interruptions of life.

We were created for meaning and depth, not just quick transactional exchanges. Without space, relationships fall apart. Friendships, marriages, and even the closest families don't thrive without unfiltered time. Quality conversation and interactions are necessary for a relationship to flourish.

In the gospels, you'll notice that Jesus says, "follow me" repeatedly. While worshipping him only requires a few hours of our schedule, following him asks a lot more of us. Everything, in fact. Following him requires all of our being, including our time, schedule, and space.

What does your spaceless life cost you? Do you feel like your spiritual life is non-existent? Do you feel like all of your relationships are hanging on by a thread or constantly in turmoil? Are you missing out on the fullness of a relationship with Jesus?

Write the simple statement "Jesus was relaxed." on a post-it and put it someplace you frequent often (bathroom mirror, desk at work, steering wheel) as a reminder that a spacious life is one of ease. Let it motivate you to continue making choices that free up space in your life.

Prayer

Jesus, someday, when we meet face to face, I'm going to ask you how you remained so relaxed with so much to do and so many people who were always in need of you. I am truly wonderstruck and I want to be more like you. Forgive me for not taking your word seriously when it says "follow me." I want my days and my demeanor to be proof that I follow you. Thank you for how you keep pointing me towards truth, growth, and inevitably, space. Amen.

Day 8
What Would You Learn Through Space in
Your Life?

People who conceal their sins will not prosper,
but if they confess and turn from them, they
will receive mercy. Proverbs 28:13

I expected God to be angry with me; to scold
and punish me. The very first night of my
solo solitude retreat, I brought all of my junk
before God and spilled truths I'd never told
anyone. I wept... apologized profusely... and
waited expectantly for a beating.

You see, I'd made mistakes. Not just small
ones like a little white lie here or a smudge
of gossip there. No, the mistakes I made
were unforgivable, I told myself.

I kept myself busy because slowing down
was when I began thinking about all I'd ever
done wrong. I didn't allow space in my life
because space meant facing my insecurities
and sin. It meant I had to sit in the company
of my own thoughts and be completely
honest with myself. That would be too
painful, I assumed.

I was right — it was painful, consciously bringing my darkness to the light, especially at first. But outweighing the pain was freedom and mercy; mercy as deep and wide as an ocean, beckoning me to plunge in head first. There was no scolding, beating or humiliation waiting for me when I confessed my sins.

In the space of my life, I have nothing to prove. All is known and all is forgiven.

Space in my life propelled me to ditch religion and participate in a real relationship with God; one that transforms me over and over and over again.

I don't know exactly what you will learn when you allow space in you life. Perhaps it will be the knowledge of who you really are; the good, the bad, and the ugly. Maybe it will be a recognition that God's mercy always prevails. You might be reminded that the world does not revolve around you. There's a possibility that you will determine your next right move. Whatever you learn here, in the

space of your life, I am confident it will transform you.
You long for space more as you grow in dependence upon the God who meets you there.

May your longing begin.

Prayer

Lord, I learn so much whenever I create and protect space in my life. I learn who I am and who I am not. You compensate for my weakness. I don't have to pretend to be strong when I'm not. You teach me how to be a human being instead of a human doing. There's so much I miss out on when I don't allow space in my days! I'm so thankful for your love and mercy. Help me to always see the value in retreating from the chaotic, noisy world. Forgive me for all of the ways I've sinned. I want to be transformed and restored. I believe this in your name. Amen.

Day 9
What Will You Hear in the Space of Your
Life?

And after the earthquake there was a fire, but the Lord was not in the fire. And after the fire there was the sound of a gentle whisper. 1 Kings 19:12

I met up with a close girlfriend for a coffee date at Starbucks around this time last year. From the moment we sat down, I immediately began offering up what was going on in my life! I spilled the good, the hard, the new, and the juicy. I spoke so fast, barely inhaling for oxygen, while rambling incessantly about every detail to catch her up on my life. My sweet friend nodded her head between bites of a blueberry scone and sips of coffee.

Suddenly, she excused herself to use the restroom. She returned to the table, mentioning how quickly an hour passed and that she really needed to head home. We hugged and parted ways. It felt abrupt. I immediately knew something was off.

I sat for a minute feeling guilty and selfish for not asking how she was. I mulled over whether or not to say something. Finally, I decided to shoot her a quick text message. In it, I apologized for taking up our entire time talking about my life. I expressed how much it meant to me that we were able to spend time together. She was kind, but also honest in her response: "I would love to have another coffee date, but I need you to know that I also have things in my life I want to share with you. You never stop talking long enough to listen."

Ouch. The words kept floating around in my head. *You never stop talking long enough to listen.* My gut feeling that something was off was right. It sucked, but oh how I needed to be smacked square in the face with truth.

The funny thing is, I wasn't only this way with my friend. I realized I'd been treating my relationship with God the same — going about my life, stopping to talk His ear off for an hour or so, and then moving on. Go, go, go. Do, do, do. Don't stop moving. Talk, talk, talk. Repeat. Where's the time to listen? To hear from God?

Since that interaction with my friend, God has continued to gently remind me that He has things he wants to share with me. I just have to stop talking, moving, and multitasking long enough to listen.

Sometimes He wants to whisper how much He loves me. Other times He nudges me toward confession. Occasionally He wants to redirect me and many times He wants to reflect with me. Regardless, it's always a gift.

Without space, we live jam-packed lives at the speed of 100mph. There's no time for reflection, recognition, or confession. Everything is a blur. We miss out.

With space, we are able to see clearly and acknowledge where we've gone off course. We are able to hear God affirming us, nudging us in a certain direction, and guiding us through the big and small moments of our daily lives.

Space to hear from people who love us and have our best interests at heart is invaluable, but space to hear from God is irreplaceable.

Pause. Quiet yourself. Stop talking long enough to listen. Don't miss out on what God wants to whisper to you today.

Prayer

Jesus, thank you for friends who are bold enough to tell the truth to us in love. Thank you for finding creative ways to teach me little lessons throughout my days. I am desperate for your grace and mercy. Please meet me in the space of my day. When I quiet myself, will you speak? Will you remind me of your love, nudge me where I need to confess, and say whatever I need to hear most? I want to be more like you. I trust you. Amen.

Day 10
How Will Your Soul Change Because of
Space?

*God doesn't come and go. God lasts. He's
Creator of all you can see or imagine. He
doesn't get tired out, doesn't pause to catch his
breath. And he knows everything, inside and
out. He energizes those who get tired, gives
fresh strength to dropouts. For even young
people tire and drop out, young folk in their
prime stumble and fall. But those who wait
upon God get fresh strength. They spread
their wings and soar like eagles, They run and
don't get tired, they walk and don't lag behind.*
Isaiah 40:30-31

Every year I go to a little cabin in the woods
of Michigan to get away from the noise and
busyness of my city life in an effort to
intentionally meet with God. The last two
times I've arrived tired and discouraged.
Despite my weariness and skepticism, God
never fails to meet me there. His Spirit
changes my soul in ways no words suffice.

Right where you're at, God longs transform
your soul. Don't buy the lie you must have

the perfect conditions to encounter the Holy Spirit.

Pay attention. What is stirring inside you? What feelings of desperation and desire flood your heart? Allow those to be the very things that motivate you to pursue time with God in solitude.

Make it your new norm. Choose a regular time and place to get away from all things life and spend a few minutes in solitude regularly. The way you've always functioned doesn't have to be the same way you continue to function.

Eliminate distractions. Anything that is distracting you from having space and being in the presence of God can be eliminated. I'm not saying to destroy your iPhone, but I am saying to eliminate it whenever possible. Turn it off, leave it in another room, disable notifications. Remember: you control the phone, the phone doesn't control you.

Let your Spirit listen when your mind can't. Recognize when you've become dangerously tired or exhausted by life's demands to the point where you can't hear God's voice speaking to you. While you're spending time in solitude, take deep breaths and let the peace of God's presence fill you. When God speaks, your Spirit can listen to what your mind can't comprehend.

Stop seeing a void as a bad thing. Don't try to deny or avoid the emptiness you feel inside sometimes. Face yourself as you really are and let God help you. Rather than hiding or denying who you are, allow the truth of who you are to surface during solitude – and face the reality of the person you see, flaws and all.

Let God fill your void. Instead of using another human being, obsessively working out, throwing back shots of Tequila or other distractions to fill your void, remember that God loves you deeply and unconditionally.

Love from a place of overflow. The love that you will experience from God in solitude will spill out into other people's lives. Take what God gives you during your quiet time with Him and use it to bless others when you're with them.

As Max Lucado once said, God loves you just as you are but also loves you too much to let you stay as you are.

The secret sauce for change is space to be in solitude with God. Position yourself to be seen, known, and loved. Show up willing, vulnerable, and teachable. Prepare to be refreshed and made new.

Prayer

Father, why would I ever choose anything over space to spend time in your presence? No other human or thing can satisfy the deep longings of my soul like you. I confess all of the ways and times I've tried to fill a void with something other than you. Thank you for loving me unconditionally and for transforming me from the inside out. Amen.

Day 11
Steps to Take Towards Space

Am I now trying to win the approval of human beings, or of God? Or am I trying to please people? If I were still trying to please people, I would not be a servant of Christ. Galatians 1:10

Toxic, negative, and codependent people wear me down and stress me out. I want space from them, but often feel bad, like it's my responsibility to just suck it up. Even when I justify my longing for space, I never know how to make it happen without hurting them in the process. Sound familiar? Any of your friends, family, classmates, or colleagues come to mind?

I admire how Jesus spent time with, taught, and healed people, all kinds of people — including toxic, negative, and codependent people. Even more so, I'm grateful for the example he set with boundaries and soul care because it gives us permission to do the same. You see, here's what I know to be true about Jesus...

Jesus did not live to please people and make them happy. He didn't always do what people wanted him to do. He made space and kept it sacred. He was not afraid to be bold and speak the truth in love. I've never met someone who claimed Jesus was selfish and yet he had a practice of space in his daily life.

Looking at his life here on earth, it's obvious he had far more stress, pressure, and responsibility than me (probably you too), yet he remained joyful, faithful and generous with people. He modeled so beautifully what it means to live with space.

Things we know about Jesus:

He didn't allow people to pull him away from what he was doing. (Matthew 12:46-50)
He wasn't always 'nice' to people; he had a backbone! (Matthew 21:12)
He fulfilled his commitments one at a time. (Mark 1:38)
He was never in a hurry. (Mark 10:32)
He withdrew from the crowds in order to spend time with God. (Luke 5:16)

He wasn't friends with everyone. (Luke 6:12-13)
He got plenty of sleep and even took naps. (Luke 8:23)

If this was how Jesus lived, I think we can trust that it was right; healthy and even holy.

Practice flexing your 'no' muscle, get plenty of rest, be present wherever you are at, speak the truth in love, and protect your time with God. Be unique - living with space - in a world where everyone is trying to avoid it.

Prayer

God, show me how to live creatively in a world where everyone tries to be the same. Help me to set boundaries so I can have space from those who drag me down without hurting them in the process. I know it's better to live for you than to spend my days trying to please everyone else. I know you have more for me than to simply be nice. Make me bold enough to take a step toward space and wise enough to keep it. Thank you for sending your son Jesus to this earth so that I could see this modeled so well. Amen.

Day 12
Declutter for More Space

He led me to a place of safety; he rescued me because he delights in me. Psalm 18:19

Are you a purger or a hoarder? Maybe a little bit of both depending on the different areas of life.

Do you clear clutter and keep making room for new or do you have a tendency to keep things for the sake of keeping them?

The older I get the more I value a spacious life.

In my environments, when I have space, I find that life is more easeful.

In my spirit, when I have space, I find that everyday moments feel more significant and impactful.

Living more spaciously has allowed God to show me that I am enough.

Creating space is a practice that humbles me, both physically and spiritually.

Every time I whittle down my closet and fill a bag for donation, I realize the abundance I live in. I let go and say thank you. In the letting go I am filled up with God's presence and peace.

Every time I whittle down my lists and commitments — especially the pressure to prove — I am reawakened to the fact this world does not revolve around me; nor does it spin because of me. I take a deep, long exhale and say thank you, Jesus.

It has been through the art of slowing down, creating space, and listening in the quiet moments that I've found God has much more to do in me than I could ever imagine.

Friend, it's a relief to know that God will continue to do good work in and through us, isn't it? There's no "level" where we are finished. We can't strive to achieve perfectionism or a life free of dependence upon Him because that life does not exist!

He is waiting for you in the quiet, open space of surrender.

What do you need to declutter in your environment and in your soul this week?

Prayer

Jesus, thank you for breathing room in my life. In my environments and especially in my soul, help me to purge everything that no longer serves a purpose or makes life messier. Whatever I need to let go of, help me to loosen my grip today. I'm sorry for the ways I cling to things and people and drama; it only keeps me further from you. I want to experience more of you and the work you are doing in me. I confess my need for space and reliance on you to help me make this a true lifestyle shift. Amen.

Day 13
Am I a Bad Person for Needing Space from Others?

If people are causing divisions among you, give a first and second warning. After that, have nothing more to do with them. Titus 3:10

One time I got burned by a close friend; a friend who was more like a sister to me. After things cooled off, we tried to mend our friendship, but within a short span of time, new problems arose.

Because I love Jesus and have experienced his grace and mercy, I've always done my best to offer that same unconditional love and grace to others. I didn't realize love and grace could actually mean space.

You see, I'd participate in the cycle of our exhausting friendship...

We communicated daily and spent tons of time together. At some point she would say something to tear me down. I'd put up with it thinking I should simply love and forgive her as Christ does for me. She would get mad at me for something. I'd apologize. We would snap right back to being close friends. Another jab or incident would crush me. I'd forgive her. We'd move on like nothing happened. Time and time again, I brought my confused and broken heart before God and asked him what the heck I was supposed to do. This relationship I felt was supposed to work just wasn't anymore.

I repeatedly asked God why he kept allowing me to get hurt. Of course, in typical God-fashion, his answer was in the form of a question back to me. "Why are you allowing this person to hurt you so much?"

Sometimes we allow ourselves to endure unnecessary wounding in relationships because we misinterpret God's word and think we're honoring Christ when in reality we're being a punching bag. We need to stop confusing the Jesus way and self-destruction!

While there are a plethora of verses throughout scripture that instruct us to take up our cross and turn the other cheek, there are just as many that remind us to apply Godly wisdom to our relationships.

I'd misinterpreted God's word and actually believed I should be "content with insults" or "suffer" to find favor with God. Essentially, I thought I was supposed to live with pain and hardships at all times and do it well.

But that's not what God wants for me, or you.

He wants boundaries to be a part of our lives. He wants us to limit the influence of toxic people in our lives. He wants us to create space for ourselves and at times, from others.

So no, you're not a bad person from needing space from others. You're human and you're wise.

Prayer

God, thank you for opening my eyes and giving my guidance when I need it most. Help me to discern when it is best for me to pull away from others. Please give me the courage to make space in my life, especially from unhealthy, toxic relationships. I know you want me to be loving and full of grace, but you also want me to own my identity as a child of God. Therefore, I will not be a doormat or a punching bag. I am so grateful for the space to reclaim my true identity. Amen.

Day 14
Use Your Space Well

Work six days. The seventh day is a Sabbath, a day of total and complete rest, a sacred assembly. Don't do any work. Wherever you live, it is a Sabbath to God. Leviticus 23:3

I used to believe Sabbath meant not doing any chores or work on Sundays. I'd get home from church, put my feet up on the couch, stuff my face with pizza, watch Netflix or scroll on my phone and call it "honoring the Sabbath."

In the words of Peter Scazzero, author of The Emotionally Healthy Leader, "Biblical sabbath is a twenty-four-hour block of time in which we stop our work, enjoy rest, practice delight, and contemplate God."

Whoa. I might not have been working, but I certainly haven't been practicing delight or contemplating God. Scrolling on Instagram or watching TV isn't all bad, but I was checking out, not honoring the Sabbath.

Sabbath is intentional space used well. It's on purpose with purpose.

I've been on a quest to figure out what it means for me to enjoy rest, practice delight, and contemplate God. I want you to start considering what it looks like for you.

Here's a sample of what my Sabbath often looks like. From Thursday evening until Saturday morning I:

- Unplug from social media.
- Stay away from emails and all things work-related.
- Focus on being in the present and look for God in all things. (I even chew my food more slowly.)
- Enjoy alone time in prayer.
- Do things that fill my tank & allow me to delight in life, such as going for a bike ride along the lake, seeing a movie by myself, or laughing hysterically over drinks with my husband. (Nothing that would be considered an obligation is allowed!)
- Don't take pictures.

What if you created your own Sabbath? What if you not only created space in your life, but used it really well?

It doesn't have to look like mine. In fact, it shouldn't. Your schedule is different. Your needs are different. Start small. Build a sacred space into the rhythm of your life. What are the things you need to do in order to actually stop work and chores for a 24-hour period? What brings your soul joy? When do you feel closest to God?

Decide. Prepare. Go there. Don't be scared to ask for help from family or friends to make it happen. You'll be amazed at how you feel, the ways your interactions shift, what God reveals, and your ability to pour into others more once you use carved out space to allow God to refuel your soul.

Prayer

Father, thank you for modeling a better way for our lives. Thank you for resting and showing me that it is good - even holy - to work hard and rest well. I'm sorry for neglecting this. Show me when and how to have this rhythm in my chaotic life. I am excited to delight in all of your creation and to be delighted by you. Amen.

Day 15
What If You Made Space for Your Emotions?

For the Spirit God gave us does not make us timid, but gives us power, love and self-discipline. 2 Timothy 1:7

When my husband and I were in the midst of parenting (we foster) the most adorable twin 3-year-old girls, I threw a shoe at the wall as hard as I could in a fit of rage.

You can't "hurt" a shoe, I know, but I had become so angry over a slew of different things in the days prior and had no time to process that anger until one morning when I LOST it.

It might sound minor to you, so let me give you a more clear picture. I didn't just chuck the shoe. I screamed. I cursed. I pushed my husband out of my way. I stomped like a mad woman. I took my fist and punched it into our bathroom door. (By the grace of God the door didn't break and neither did my hand.) I saw red; anger to the point of rage. In the audience of my act stood our two beautiful, precious girls, completely traumatized. I felt so guilty and ashamed afterwards. Today the most maddening thing about it is that I can't even remember what triggered my explosion. All I recall is a bunch of my feelings compounding until I flew off the handle.

It's like shaking a bottle of soda really hard. Twist the cap off a little bit, really slowly, and there will be a release. However, if you twist the cap off all of the way, without caution, after shaking it really hard - WATCH OUT!

I'm the bottle of soda, dear reader. *And I wonder if sometimes you are too?*

Without little releases along the way, everyday, our emotions compound until suddenly, over something small — like your husband not hanging up his wet towel or your kid spilling a cup of milk by accident — we explode.

It wasn't until I made a decision that I was going to work on everyday little releases that I started noticing a drastic decrease in my small fits of anger.

I think staying busy and living without space is how so many of us cope. But what if there's a better way? What if we made space for our emotions and allowed them to be a gauge in our lives?

Our emotions were meant to report to us, not rule us.

The pattern of our emotions will give us an honest reading on where our hope lies because they are tied to what we believe and value, and how much. They come up a lot in the Bible because emotions reveal what our hearts love, trust, and fear!

Let's stop running from them. Instead, let's make space in our lives to face them and use them for good.

Starting today, make space to write about your feelings, talk through them and express them creatively. You'll learn a lot about yourself this way and avoid those embarrassing, harmful explosions.

Prayer

Heavenly Father, thank you for giving me emotions and feelings. Thank you for helping me learn how to manage and deal with them in healthy ways. I'm sorry for how I've allowed what I feel at times to dictate my life choices — big and small. Please reveal to me all I am trying to avoid by staying busy. My hope is in you! I ask that your Spirit would give me power, love, and self-discipline. Make me brave enough to face the feelings at war inside my body. Amen.

Day 16
Will You Make Space for Spontaneity?

Many are the plans in a person's heart, but it is the Lord's purpose that prevails. Proverbs 19:21

I grew up believing that being constantly busy was normal. I filled whatever space I had without even realizing what I was doing. It became an unconscious pattern that led me to have an overwhelmed schedule with an underwhelmed soul.

I'd been a planner and a list maker my whole life so when I decided space was something I needed to get serious about, I didn't stop planning and list making; I just learned to infuse my plans and lists with space; space for spontaneity, whim, something unimaginable.

The idea of planning for spontaneity sounds silly, I know, but have you ever had an opportunity you really wanted to take only to realize your day was already full with prior obligations? Do you move from task to task without room to pause, think, or breathe? Have you found yourself saying "I'm too busy" or often telling the people you love, "I'm sorry, I just don't have time."

When I imagine myself at the end of my life (hopefully on the beach with my husband), I wonder what my future self would say to me smack dab in the midst of "the good ol' days" we are in right now? What secrets would she whisper? What regrets would she have?

Of course, there's no way of knowing for sure, but I imagine she'd say:

Make space for spontaneity. Don't hold life and your precious plans too closely. God always has something better than you expect, better than you could have planned. Hug your people longer. Don't rush off without kissing your husband like you mean it. Show up for your friends and tell them how proud you are of them. Always choose people over productivity. Get lost in time doing things you love with people you love. Always leave space for the unimaginable.

I dare you to join me.

Choose a chunk of time in your day and schedule it to be unscheduled. Reserve space for something unexpected and delightful to happen.

Honor your weekends. They can fill up with bridal showers, baby showers, weddings, home projects, family reunions, and other commitments all too quickly. Designate at least one weekend each month solely for rest and play.

Unplug. I don't think we could ever underestimate how much time we waste online. Ditch the phone (social media, email, texts, voicemails, pictures, etc.) and reclaim your time and space.

Some of the most powerful experiences in life are unplanned and well within our reach. Let's make space for spontaneity; the freedom to follow our intuition and collide with God in the unexpected.

Prayer

God, thanks for reminding me just how small I am in the grand scheme of this world. I'm amazed that you know the exact number of hairs on my head or grains of sand that exist. What a relief that you are so much wiser, more knowledgeable and powerful than me. I don't have to always have everything planned out and figured out. Help me to follow where your Spirit leads. I want to make space for spontaneity... for fun, unexpected encounters and delight. I love you and I'm so grateful. Amen.

Day 17
Who Are You When You Have Space?

*Yet God, in His grace, freely makes us right in
his sight. He did this through Christ Jesus
when he freed us from the penalty for our
sins.* Romans 3:24

Here's who I am when I have space in my life:

More aware. Space allows the chaos that's
deep in my soul to surface. I always say, "You
don't know what you don't know," so having
breathing room allows me to face what I
would otherwise be oblivious to in the frenzy
of everyday life.

Healthier. Space reveals the Lord's remedy
for my deepest fears, wounds, and ongoing
struggles. I tend to make wiser choices and
react to people and circumstances much
better when I'm living at a pace that allows
for space in my days.

More confident and peaceful. Space gives
me time with, and to hear from, my loving
Father. I'm reminded that I am worthy, loved

and forgiven. There's a confidence and a peace that comes with that heart knowledge.

Growing and transforming. Space is where God reveals things I don't want to acknowledge or have avoided completely. It helps me to know myself better, rely on God more, and do the next right thing.

Space has become essential to my being. Without it, I'm not only unaware, unhealthy, full of shame, and not at ease — I'm stuck. On the contrary, with space, I constantly begin over again. It's a beautiful thing, having a million second chances and fresh starts to move forward.

Space is a vital part of my relationship with Jesus and, quite possibly, the secret sauce to my transformation in Him.

Who are you when you have space?

Take a few minutes to ponder, reflect and journal about it.

Prayer

Lord, I haven't had as much space in my life as I know I need. I'm so sorry for getting caught up in the world's standards of time, hustle, relationships, and cultural norms. Forgive me for not honoring you with my days and wasting time by trying to do it all without you. I want to be a beautiful representation of your transforming grace. When I think I don't need space, or it's lacking in my life, help pull me back. Thank you for your relentless pursuit of my heart and soul. Amen.

Day 18
Could Space Save Your Relationship?

Be kind and compassionate to one another, forgiving each other, just as in Christ God forgave you. Ephesians 4:32

I wasn't getting along with one of my closest friends. Although she stood by my side on my wedding day five years ago, we weren't exempt from relational strife.

Ultimately, space saved our relationship. You see, people change with time. Since we first became friends eight years ago, I changed and so had she. We had both graduated from college, I got married, we both moved, she started seeing someone new, we both changed jobs and started having new friends in our lives, and I became a foster mom.

Neither of us were doing anything wrong, we were just in very different phases of life with less in common, including schedules. We began having a harder time relating to one another and our relationship required more effort than it used to.

I also didn't feel comfortable saying "Hey, that really hurt my feelings..." or "Can you support me by ____?" The idea of being totally transparent or giving her the opportunity to be the kind of friend I needed was scary. *What if she let me down?*

I now know how crucial it is to be transparent and face the awkwardness of being real in relationships rather than faking fine. But at a time I wasn't capable or ready to do so, space saved my friendship.

After some heated confrontations she and I swept everything under the rug and casually went back to being "good" friends. Unfortunately, this only created animosity between us.

It wasn't until we took some time to be apart and that we both were able to see things clearly. In the space, I was able to determine my needs, wants, and expectations. I was able to filter my feelings, find the truth and articulate it with her in a mature way.

We both recognized life was too short to hold grudges and it was far too short to pretend we were OK when we weren't. We made a pact to always be honest with each other and to speak up if we weren't respecting each other's boundaries.

Moral of the story: temporary space may be what saves your relationship.

Don't be afraid to let somebody miss you while you work on you. Use the space well. Bring your concerns and angst to Jesus. Decide what you are willing to put in going forward. Most of all, be kind and compassionate. Forgive others just like God forgives you.

Prayer

Heavenly Father, thank you for your mercy. Sometimes it's hard for me to believe I'm fully forgiven and wholly loved. I don't deserve your grace, but Lord, help me to delight in the freedom that it brings and to never withhold that from anyone else. I want to offer grace and forgiveness and space in all of my relationships so they bring me joy and peace, but more importantly so they honor you. Please help me to navigate conflict and hardships with others well. Amen.

Day 19
Find Your Purpose in The Space of Your Life

He lets me rest in green meadows; he leads me beside peaceful streams. He renews my strength. He guides me along right paths, bringing honor to his name. Psalm 23:2-3

Doing what we have always done will result in getting what we have always gotten.

If you feel unhappy, exhausted or unfulfilled; if you are sure that you have more to offer the world than your day to day requires of you, it's time to pause and discover your purpose. To do that, you need space in your life.

Nobody is coming along with a magical pill, a radical job offer, or a winning lottery ticket to pull you out of your life and replant you. Only you have the power to change— with God's help.

You see, God wants to give you a purpose. The Holy Spirit wants to pour wisdom over you. God isn't holding out on you to make you miserable. His desire is that you would have a joyful, ambitious, purposeful life. Ask God for purpose and expect Him to give it to you.

God often speaks to us through His word. Start digging into scripture. Now, you aren't going to find any verses that tell you, "Quit your job and apply for American Idol" (wouldn't it be nice if it were that easy?), but you will begin to understand his heart.

What strengths and gifts has God has given you? Maybe you are a great baker, painter, or the person everyone comes to for advice. Maybe you have a knack for interior decorating or photography. Perhaps you love all things business or accounting. God's purpose for you likely involves the things you're already good at, so use your strengths to lead the way.

If money wasn't part of the conversation, what would you love to do? What keeps you up at night? This can be anything... alleviating poverty, producing music, educating the next generation, baking beautiful cakes, seeing people overcome addiction, etc. The sky's the limit. What unique passion lives inside of you?

God's word reminds us that two heads are better than one and guidance keeps us from going awry. Do you have a counselor, mentor, professor, supervisor, parent, or friend you can lean into and trust? Everyone needs someone who has their back and wants the best for them. Lean into the wise, trusted people in your life as you navigate change instead of doing this on your own.

Carve out some space and time to get away from your routine. Use the unhurried space of solitude to think, pray and journal. Practice being still with God. Listen for His voice. God's not hiding in the dark, trying to keep his will hidden from you. He wants to guide you.

Get in the quiet space of your life and meet God there. He's waiting for you. You may feel confused, but God doesn't. Nothing surprises him and nothing is wasted.

Prayer

Father, thank you for bringing me into this world for a purpose. Thank you for putting gifts and passions inside of me. Thank you for the people in my life who want what's best for me. I'm so sorry that I often choose the easy way to comfort and stability rather than trusting you and taking risks that reveal my trust in you. I am going to spend time in your presence and expect you to show up. I need to be renewed and guided. Please help me to have clarity on tangible next steps and the courage to take them so I can honor you. Amen.

Day 20
Five Easy Ways to Increase Space in Your Life

I am the vine; you are the branches. If you remain in me and I in you, you will bear much fruit; apart from me you can do nothing. John 15:5

Take inventory of who you allow in your face. Take a good hard look at your social media feed, phone contacts, incoming emails — everything that's in your face. *Whose voice are you allowing to take up your space and feed your soul?* Don't be afraid to hit the unfollow, delete, or unsubscribe button. Be guarded with who gets in front of your face, even through the phone.

Schedule 15-minute breaks. I started putting 15-minute breaks on my calendar in between meetings, events, or errands as an experiment. As it turns out, I ALWAYS need those extra minutes to wrap up the last thing or just to breathe and arrive at the next unhurried. It feels good to walk into every encounter with a clear mind. (I'm also a lot more friendly this way.)

Use a proactive approach. I never used to take personal or sick days. I hustled and kept my days full, thinking I had to prove myself as the hardest worker in all the land. I bought my own lies that personal and sick days are for the weak. I've learned that they are actually for the wise. Mental health days and time away from productivity is so good for the soul. Be proactive. Schedule your time off work, projects, and parenting in advance.

Treat your time with God like an appointment you wouldn't cancel. Instead of wishing you spent more time reading your Bible or praying or going for a walk to notice God's creation all around you, make it a daily appointment and don't cancel. (You wouldn't cancel on your boss or a hot date, would you?) Don't rush through it. God's word can't soak in if we are in a hurry.

Prepare your "no speech." For a long time I wasn't sure how to turn something or someone down. Now whenever someone says, "We should grab coffee or hang out soon!" and my schedule is super full or I don't have the capacity for a new friend, I reply differently. I prepared a "no" speech and it goes a little something like this:

"I'd love to, but when I say yes and fill my schedule to the brim, I'm ultimately saying no to my husband and other people in my life who I love. In an effort to balance my time and energy, I'm scaling back and won't be able to schedule with you. I hope you understand and hear my heart on this. It's not personal. I just have to protect my space for the wellbeing of my soul."

Notice I don't apologize and I don't offer a date four months out to schedule. We, women, don't need to say sorry nearly as often as we do. In this case, there's nothing to be sorry for. Also, I don't need to schedule anything four months in advance if my next free date is four months from now. Period.

Not one time has anyone been obviously upset by my "no speech." I think most people really respect it and admire me for being cautious with my time. I believe the same will be true for you, too. Feel free to steal mine or write your own, but do it and keep it saved in the notes of your phone for easy copy-paste access. I'm serious! You're going to need it.

Prayer

Dear God, thank you for being so approachable. I'm sorry for the days I'm overly confident or complacent. Keep me humble and hungry for more of you. I want to be wise with my time and yeses. Help me give you my first yes and always prioritize you first. I long to be more intentional with space in my life because I want to bear fruit, which doesn't happen apart from you. Amen.

Day 21
Why Are You Really Avoiding Space?

Be strong and courageous. Do not be afraid or terrified because of them, for the Lord your God goes with you; he will never leave you nor forsake you. Deuteronomy 31:6

I'm the kind of person who never gets sick and when I do, I push through it going about my day as normal. I avoid laying low and really don't like falling behind when there is much to be done. So you can imagine how hard it was for me the first time I got so sick my body literally wouldn't move. I was so ill I couldn't get out of bed, though you can be sure I tried. I was forced to do nothing. It was as if God was giving me every obvious sign that I needed to simply rest in the space of life.

It's ironic how we as a society shame those who are addicted to drugs and alcohol, but somehow we normalize and rationalize — even applaud — those who are addicted to being busy.

If this were harmless, I wouldn't be so passionate about it. However, I believe busy is a drug many of us are addicted to. It's a distraction so we don't have to face what's going on below the surface; and it's holding us back from living the life God has for us.

Why have you made yourself so insanely busy? Why are you really avoiding space?

In the space of our lives, we come face to face with ourselves and the not so pretty parts of life. In the stillness of our lives we notice things we don't want to deal with; things that would be much easier to avoid by staying busy.

Here are some of the things that come up for me in the space of my life:

→ The realization of an unmet expectation in my marriage.

→ Sadness I feel due to missing the twins (our former foster daughters).

→ How uncomfortable I am when I'm not producing.

→ Guilt I feel for not spending more time with my sick grandparents.

→ The uncertainty of my own authenticity.

→ Fear that I'm missing out on something awesome. *Or even worse, that I wasn't invited.*

Yet time and time again I prescribe the 'busy' drug so that my disease lays dormant and I can go on without getting vulnerable or facing unsettling truths about myself.

But God calls us to a life so much richer than one spent busying ourselves and avoiding hard things. His word reminds us that He is there for us. We don't have to be afraid because he will never leave us. We can be brave, facing these things that surface in the space of our lives.

Spend a few minutes being honest with yourself today. What are you avoiding or hiding behind your stuffed calendar and to-do lists?

Prayer

Lord, I admit that I have an addiction and need your help to overcome it. I don't want to live busy just to avoid pain in my life. You are a healer and I long to lean on you and trust that what your word says is true – that you will never leave or abandon me. I commit to more space in my life and paying attention to why I'm avoiding it. I commit to running to you when I am tempted to busy myself. Thank you for being a solid foundation I can stand on. Amen.

Day 22
Do You Want to Grow?

Let your roots grow down into him, and let your lives be built on him. Then your faith will grow strong in the truth you were taught, and you will overflow with thankfulness.
Colossians 2:7

A few summers ago I was helping a friend do some work in her yard. While planting shrubs and flowers along her adorable home, she reminded me how important it was that I intentionally space them out. "Plants need room to grow so they can bloom and thrive," she said.

It got me thinking... so do I.

When I reflect on my life and the times I've grown the most, it was not when everything was a blur and I was moving a mile a minute. It was not when other people or my to-do lists ruled my schedule. In fact, those are the times I've felt smothered and stressed.

I grow most when I have space to learn and make mistakes. Whenever I give myself

time to try new things, explore foreign places, read new books, breathe, pray, and get in tune with myself, I grow. The most significant growth I've experienced has occurred in the space of discomfort, newness, or accountability.

The space in our life is where the magic of GROWTH happens.

Remove distractions that get in the way of who you are and what you want to do. It's tough to move if you have something weighing you down, holding you back, or getting in the way. This isn't just physical either, the emotional baggage we carry around is just as crippling.

Look inward; notice things that get missed in the busyness of your life. It feels vulnerable because it is. But it's important to do the inner work if you want to grow.

Try something you could possibly fail at. I'm guessing something comes to mind... have you always wanted to run a half-marathon? Have you always wanted to write a children's book? Have you always wanted to perform stand-up comedy? You probably haven't because of the lack of time and space in your life. But now that you are creating space by carving out time, what's holding you back? Choose faith over fear.

Seek accountability. Share this with a friend and tell them you really want to grow this season. Tell them you need more space in your life and have goals you want to see through. Be specific. Ask them for help and accountability to see it through.

Be patient. Growth doesn't happen overnight and living a life that has space might be a brand new concept for you. Like God's word reminds us, "His mercies are new every morning." There's no limited amount of restarts, so we can be gracious with ourselves when we take a step backwards.

Not only will a spacious life lead to growth. It will allow us to help others bloom too! That's what God wants for you and me, but we have to make time and space for Him if that's ever going to happen.

Prayer

God, I'm sorry for not leaving space for you. I'm sorry for trying to rush growth and cut corners. Forgive me for thinking I can reach my full potential without you. I long to have more space in my life to bloom and thrive. I long to see others I love flourishing, too. Help me to start a ripple effect by doing this well and encouraging others to do the same. I love you and can't wait to see what growth occurs as I open myself to more possibilities of your work to be done. Amen.

Day 23
11 Tips to Protect Your Space

Let us not become weary in doing good, for at the proper time we will reap a harvest if we do not give up. Galatians 6:9

#1 Pencil it in. Carve out blocks of time on your calendar just for space. If things come up (as they always do!) and the only slots you have open are during times you already blocked for space, then you are going to have to pass or that thing is going to have to wait.

#2 Create your Sabbath and honor it fiercely. Scripture puts it on the same list as murder, yet somehow we think we're exempt. Having a set aside Sabbath is not only a command from God to teach us to trust Him; it's His gift to us, so we don't become slaves to our schedules.

#3 Refuse to feel guilty. Figure out what refreshes you and learn how to lean into it more frequently! Unapologetically throw yourself into a hobby. Take a nap. Do what you need to do to stay healthy for the long-haul.

#4 Do what makes you crave more space. I've found that reaching for a good novel helps me to relax and enjoy space, which results in me craving more of it. Doing what I love in the space of my life that leaves me feeling good is undeniably the easiest way to keep on fighting for it.

#5 Take on fewer meetings. The outcome of most meetings is action items. The more meetings you are in, the fewer amount of minutes you have in a day to actually get stuff done. Make sure you have a really good reason to show up. Otherwise, don't take it on.

#6 Check your notifications less. The more you respond within minutes to every little inquiry, the more you are programming everyone to expect that from you. Remove every single beep, buzz, or interruptive alert that you receive when you get a new notification.

#7 Spend time with God daily. When you make God your first priority, everything else falls into place much easier. When you put God first, He will give you the wisdom, strength, and guidance you need to have a day that is peaceful and easeful.

#8 Cook in bulk. Whenever I cook, I do my best to duplicate the meal. I freeze extras for a day when I can really use the extra time saved or to have on hand so that I can bless someone else when they could use it.

#9 Flex your "no" muscle. Remember that "no" isn't a bad word and every time you say "no", you are actually saying "yes" to something better. Your sanity, your health, your relationships... your one precious life.

#10 Avoid duplicates in your schedule. Just because a small group at church is on your priority list doesn't mean you should do two of them. Don't try to be everything for everyone. Set your own personal cap and stick to it.

#11 Turn on your read receipt. Having it on helps me to be more conscious with text messages and communication. I only open and read them when I know I have time to reply right then and there. Otherwise, I end up reading it, often forgetting to respond, or reading it more than once until I finally reply, which adds up to wasted time and space.

Prayer

Father God, I am working so hard to make changes in my life. I ask that you guide me and send your Spirit to lead me as I fight to maintain a rhythm of space in my life. Thank you for the promises in your word. I don't want to become weary in doing good or too busy for good distractions, like the people you place in my path. Help me to pay attention and live with intentionality so that my space is protected and I am in tune with you. Amen.

Day 24
Could Space Bring Out Your Creative Side?

The heavens declare the glory of God; the skies proclaim the work of his hands. Psalm 19:1

I believe everyone is an artist.

Everyone is made in God's image and he's the biggest creative and most talented artist I've ever known. Just look at the sunset, the ocean, your closest friends!

I often hear, "I'd love to do that, but I'm not creative." In fact, I used to say that myself. I was so scared of what others might think that I kept all of my ideas and unique forms of expression to myself for many years. Even my writing was never intended for the public eye.

Back when my blog was just my anonymous online diary, I felt God prompting me to share one specific article. I posted it to Facebook scared. Turns out God knew what he was doing because it was through the prompting of his Spirit and a lot of affirmation from others that I continued to write and bravely stopped keeping it all tucked away.

The capacity to create exists within each of us. You might be a medical student, math teacher, lawyer, or accountant. You might call yourself "anything but creative," but I'm willing to bet you're wrong. Creativity is in your DNA. God passed it down to you. When you use it, you glorify Him.

Creativity can look like a whole bunch of different things — painting, cooking, photography, organizing, sewing, decorating, putting together outfits, reading, writing, playing music, collecting things... the list goes on and on.

The problem I've run into, however, is that I am not able to be creative when my life doesn't have space.

A wise person in my life recently told me, "If you wait to start creating until the dishes are done, you're caught up at work, and everyone's happy with you, you'll never start." I've found it to be so true. Space is a necessary ingredient for creative juice.

Space says the laundry can wait and no one should be working 60 hours a week.

Space invites us to do something purely for enjoyment; nonproductive fun.

Space reads a few pages in a novel or writes a few pages of our own.

Space finds us dancing in the kitchen with our person or getting our hands covered in paint or dirt with no regard for time.

This is something we will have to work at every day, but it's worth it. God intended you to live big, wild and free. He delights in you when you glorify him through creative expression. He longs for your life to be spacious so that you can channel your inner artist child.

The question is: are you ready?

Prayer

Lord, you are so creative. I look at the billions of people in this world - the way they look, how they choose to dress, the gifts you've given them, how their minds work so uniquely - and I'm in awe. I look at the stars in the sky, the waves in the ocean, and the colors of each sunrise and sunset amazed by your work. I know that as a child of God I am creative. I want to bring honor and glory to your name by tapping into my creative gifts more. Help me to do whatever I need to so that I have space in my life. Thank you for being such a fun God. Amen.

Day 25
Space for Your Health

Didn't you realize that your body is a sacred place, the place of the Holy Spirit? Don't you see that you can't live however you please, squandering what God paid such a high price for? The physical part of you is not some piece of property belonging to the spiritual part of you. God owns the whole works. So let people see God in and through your body. 1 Corinthians 6:20

A few months ago I discovered clean beauty. After learning just how bad the majority of cheap drugstore products are for my skin and overall health, I decided to purge my skincare line and make-up to replace it all with clean, toxic-free products. I was so excited and told everyone I knew so that they could make the switch too. Then, one day, a friend privately said to me, "You are taking such good care of your skin. I love that, but what about the rest of you?"

You see, she knew I ate McDonalds more often than I should, skipped lunch whenever I got too busy at work, filled up on Oreos every night with little self-control, and rarely had the energy to work-out.

At first, I got defensive, but I knew she was right. I was appalled at the thought of putting toxic chemicals on my skin, but somehow I hadn't been concerned that I consumed crazy amounts of artificial sugar and preservatives. I filled up on things out of convenience, disregarding how little they nourish my body, which is pretty much the only way to survive when you don't have space in your life.

Without space, I would continue rushing from one place to the next relying on McDonald's drive-thru. Without space, I'd continue smashing a package of Oreos each week because stress-eating is real. Without space, I wouldn't have any energy left to go running or to take a yoga class.

So, I made a choice. I wasn't going to attempt another Whole30 challenge. I wasn't going to give up Oreos or McDonalds indefinitely. I wasn't going to sign-up for a personal trainer. My choice: space.

I don't need anything other than space in my life to improve my diet and take care of my body. I can come up with all of the excuses in the world, but really if I have freed up my schedule, this isn't all that difficult.

Space in my life to grocery shop, meal prep, and sit down for lunch instead of rushing to grab fast-food or starving myself. Space in my life to sleep a little more, leave work at a decent hour, and get a run in. Space in my life to breathe, pray, pause and even cry it out when I feel stressed or overwhelmed.

I began to get rid of some things that were on my plate, say no to new things that came my way, and stick to hard boundaries with work and other people in order to free up my daily life. The result has been gold. I'm a less-stressed, healthier version of myself.

What is your body aching for? *Maybe more sleep, taking the stairs, or greens in your diet.*

Can other people tell you take care of your body like it's a true gift from God?

May your decisions to pursue health be a testament of your faith.

Prayer

God, thank you for giving me friends and people who are brave enough to call me up and hold me accountable. Thank you for giving me easy access to clean water and nourishing foods. Too often I take for granted my health and all you have provided. I want to honor you with my body in every way. Keep me from choosing the convenient, temporary-feel-good option. Teach me self-discipline, but mostly teach me to slow down so I can experience life to the fullest. My body is another way for people to see Christ in me. Let me treat it so. Amen.

Day 26
Does Space Have Any Impact on My Finances?

No one can serve two masters. Either you will hate one and love the other, or you will be devoted to the one and despise the other. You cannot serve both God and money. Matthew 6:24

Living a life that is overly full and fast-paced normally causes me to make poor decisions. Often times the consequence of these decisions are reflected on my bank statements.

When I'm swamped I swipe my card more.

I swipe because I'm in a hurry and I need to eat on the go. I swipe because I'm stressed and retail therapy lures me in. I swipe because I'm bored and I'd rather fill the time with doing something more fun than sitting in the space. The impact on my finances is real.

Money tends to be a wonky subject. Many couples fight about it and most people wish they had more of it. I've seen it destroy friendships and make dreams come to life.

Whenever I'm tempted to believe I'd be happier if I had more money, I think about some of the richest people in this world and how unhappy they are. I think about how many suicides that took place in the last year were people at the top of the economic ladder. I reflect on those whose hearts worship money; complaining even when someone gives them a substantial gift because it's never enough.

We don't need more money or stuff to enjoy our lives. We need more wisdom and discipline to ensure we use what he gives us for his glory. I'm convinced we can get there with space.

Space to recognize all of the blessings around us.

Space to thank God for always providing what we need.

Space to acknowledge that he is a God of abundance.

Space to do things other than shop when we are hurting.

Space to hear the Spirit whisper and discern our every purchase.

Maybe spending frivolously has become a bad habit; a thing you do to fill a void in your soul.

Maybe living paycheck to paycheck is all you have ever known; a cycle you can't seem to break. Or maybe you long to be generous, but never have space in your budget for spontaneous generosity; a discipline you have been avoiding.

Ask yourself the hard questions: Do I serve God or money? Does my lifestyle reflect this?

Let's give back to God what is already His and practice giving joyfully as we increase the space in all areas of our lives.

Prayer

Heavenly Father, I'm sorry that I struggle with loving money and wanting more of it. Thank you for pulling my heart in the opposite direction whenever I start to worship and idolize it above you and others. Your word is clear and I don't want to serve anything except for you. You have been so, so good to me. Help me to be wise with my finances and resources. Help me to live a life that has space for wherever you are calling me to, generosity towards my friends, and trust that there's enough for me today. Amen.

Day 27
Gratitude in the Space of Your Life

Give thanks in all circumstances; for this is God's will for you in Christ Jesus. 1 Thessalonians 5:18

Can you recall a time in your life when the days felt so mundane, depressing, or blurry? Perhaps you are currently in season like that?

With the ongoing demands of paying bills and keeping up with household chores, all while caring for ourselves and others, we are often left exhausted, grumpy, and unfulfilled.

Maybe like me, you desire a life that is slower; one where you are more present and end your nights feeling deeply fulfilled.

A life without gratitude will often feel shallow, purposeless, and underwhelming. It doesn't matter what your job title is, how much you have achieved, if you are well-known, or have a lot of zero's tagged on your bank account.

Space is often a springboard for my gratitude.

That gratitude is not limited to a holiday that occurs once each year. God wants us to be intentional about our thankfulness every single day. He wants us to develop this spiritual habit of thanking Him in all circumstances.

I know it sounds crazy — thanking God when sucky situations arise that are completely out of our control; like when you lose a job, or a friend, or a diagnosis is made that you can't wrap your brain around, but friend, God is always working to bring good out of hard things. He can redeem the stupid mistakes you have made or the tough thing that just happened in your life. No matter what, He will never stop loving you. And the truth is: there are a hundred things to be thankful for in all circumstances, even when the circumstance blows.

Who do you wish you were closer with? Does a friend come to mind or maybe your significant other? Do what you did when you were first friends or newly dating — express your gratitude for them in a million little ways!

Write encouraging notes. Pick up the phone and call because you care. Go out of your way to show them how much they mean to you. Let your gratitude be felt through the space in your life to show up for them.

As you develop an attitude of gratitude, what changes do you think you might see in yourself and all of your relationships?

Prayer

Jesus, forgive me for not paying attention. Forgive me for being so wrapped up in my own little world that I miss the most beautiful opportunities to express my gratitude. I am so undeserving of all you provide and redeem in my life. Thank you for changing my heart. I believe you are worthy of my thanks in all circumstances. I want my gratitude to be over the top, constant, and overflowing so that it reaches everyone I encounter. Amen.

Day 28
Time to Quit Something!

There is a time for everything, and a season for every activity under the heavens: a time to be born and a time to die, a time to plant and a time to uproot, a time to kill and a time to heal, a time to tear down and a time to build, a time to weep and a time to laugh, a time to mourn and a time to dance, a time to scatter stones and a time to gather them, a time to embrace and a time to refrain from embracing, a time to search and a time to give up, a time to keep and a time to throw away, a time to tear and a time to mend, a time to be silent and a time to speak, a time to love and a time to hate, a time for war and a time for peace. Ecclesiastes 3:1-8

There's an author who's on my dinner wishlist. Bob Goff. *You may have heard of him.* Let me backup in case you're wondering what my dinner wishlist is. It's the list of people I would love to have dinner with before I die.

So why did Bob Goff make my list over Beyonce? Easy. Bob is a New York Times

Best-Selling Author and the founder of a nonprofit human rights organization called Love Does, which operates in Uganda, India, Iraq, Nepal, Afghanistan and Somalia. He's a sought after speaker and easily one of the most accomplished people I have ever heard of. But none of that stuff is my real reason for wanting to have dinner with him.

Over the years of reading his books, listening to his talks, and following his journey online, it's undeniable that Bob seems to enjoy life more than most people. He never stops smiling. From what everyone says about him, he's genuinely happy and kind all of the time.

While there's a plethora of things to attribute Bob's incredible success in life, including his happy and kind demeanor which can't hurt, there's an unconventional method he shares publicly that I believe is a big reason he remains so joyful rather than stressed out: Bob quits one thing every Thursday.

Yes, it's as straightforward as it sounds. Every week (specifically on Thursday), he quits one thing.

Why?

We all do things we don't need to be doing, according to Bob. (For the record, I agree!)

We do things that drain our energy, passion, and crowd our lives so much that we have no space left and can't do the amazing things we should be putting all of our energy and passion into.

I may not be able to have dinner and dig deep with Bob anytime soon, but I have followed in his footsteps and started quitting things each week to make room for what really matters in my life.

Join us, won't you? What is one thing you can throw out of your life for good that will help you be happier, more focused, fulfilled, and better able to accomplish what your real calling in life is?

Go with your gut. Don't go too big. Don't overthink it.

I double dare you to share this with someone you trust. Tell them what you decided to quit forever so that you can have more space in your life!

Prayer

God, what are you calling me to? What have you prepared me for? What do I need to quit? I am so thankful for how you use ordinary people to do extraordinary things. I surrender my story because I know you will write a better one. Help me to sit in the quiet of space and listen for direction from you. Amen.

Day 29
A Change of Pace, a Change of Heart

Have I not commanded you? Be strong and courageous. Do not be afraid; do not be discouraged, for the Lord your God will be with you wherever you go. Joshua 1:9

In the Fall of 2017, my husband and I received our first child through foster care.

What was supposed to be one little girl for a short 2-week placement wound up being twin toddlers that stayed in our care for nearly 9 months. It was hard, wonderful, messy and beautiful.

A lot of things changed, but my pace of living took the biggest hit.

Before having these twin 3-year-old girls, I could run all over town, stay up till the wee hours in the morning tackling a project, and rush out the door on a last minute notice. I was a girl on the run, at all times.

Once we got the twins, I could no longer buzz around town doing whatever I wanted.

Even if I did have a full day, it was much slower. There were two more bodies to buckle up. They needed me to teach them how to stop pooping their pants and so much more (although it felt like potty-training was the only thing for a long while). They demanded my attention in every way. I could no longer spend my days going from thing to thing because life revolved around their needs.

Suddenly, I had to find alternatives, make do with less free time, and determine if it was worth the hassle to do whatever we were going to do because you can't take Ubers when your children are still in car-seats and need their nap time (even if just for your sanity).

My pace went from 10000 mph to 5 mph and it wrecked me. At times, this pace of life made me frustrated. Now, I can clearly see it was some of the best work God has done in my heart. It's when he revealed what really mattered most in this life.

I learned (reluctantly) what it meant to have space in the midst of my life feeling very full.

Your pace will change as life ebbs and flows. Sometimes a change of pace will force space in, whether you want it or not.

Maybe you just lost your job or you just had a baby. Perhaps something else has happened and you find yourself navigating a new pace. Embrace it, friend. God is with you.

This is the space that transforms your heart in ways you didn't know you needed.

Prayer

Jesus, my life is shifting and my pace is changing. I want to navigate it well and to do so, I need you now more than ever. Help me to seek you when I feel slow and frustrated. Forgive me for missing out on the good stuff that's right in front of my face. Help me to seek you when life is fast and frantic. Thank you for revealing yourself and your love for me in the space of my days. I will keep returning for more of you. Amen.

Day 30
Encourage Others to Unwrap the Gift of
Space

Do not withhold good from those who deserve
it when it's in your power to help them.
Proverbs 3:27

Erin Loechner, a writer I deeply admire and
resonate with, wrote this brilliant line in her
book *Chasing Slow*, "Here is the secret to
subtraction. It doesn't matter what you
remove. What matters is that you stop
adding it back."

When I first read this, I felt super convicted
because I have a tendency to remove things
from my life pretty easily, but just as simply
as I remove something, I replace it with
another thing. This is especially true for my
calendar.

One of the ways I've sustained my
transformation on this journey to living with
space is by sharing my goals and desires
publicly and with close friends who lovingly
hold me accountable.

After sharing my venture to have more space in my life, a friend started checking in on my weekends specifically. She pointed out and celebrated my progress. She said before this journey she had never witnessed me go an entire weekend without places to be or people to see. It made me laugh. She was right. (And it was one of the best weekends in such a long time.)

I'm lighter, freer, and more connected to God who is ever-present in my spacious days. I so badly want the same to be true for you.

When someone asks how you are doing, I pray you no longer answer with "busy." I hope you eliminate it from your vocabulary as you cut things out of your life.
People really do want to know how your heart is doing when they ask how you are. So tell them.

Tell them your heart is joyous or that your heart is aching.
Tell them your heart is sad, if it is, and let them know what your heart needs.

Tell them you are a human being, not just a human doing.
Tell them you are really living, not just producing.
Pause to have that conversation.
Full of healing and grace and presence.
Look them in the eye and connect.
Tell them something true about your heart so you may awaken theirs in the process.

Space in our lives will not guarantee a life free of problems or conflict, but it will change our soul and have a ripple effect on those around us. I promise because I'm in it with you, seeing this unfold in my own life.

Let's take the space we fight so hard for and use it well, allowing our transformation to transform others.

Invite someone you love to unwrap this gift that eagerly awaits them.

Prayer

Lord, I am so thankful for 30 days of intentionally seeking you. In the fight for space, I know you are fighting for my soul.

Thank you for lifting me up, reaching me in the most unexpected ways, and loving me too much to leave me where I am. Let my life be an encouragement to others. Keep drawing me in deeper through every little bit of silence and nothingness in my days. I love you more than my words could ever express. Amen.

Discussion Questions:

1. Your mind lies, but your body cannot lie. This is the most beautiful gift from God. Pay attention. When your mind says you're OK, but your gut is reeking with anxiety, you might need space. *What is your body trying to tell you today?*

2. Using your space well means checking in vs numbing out. To me, numbing out often looks like: scrolling mindlessly, binge-watching or eating, cleaning incessantly, and venting or gossiping. Meanwhile, checking in looks like: reading a book, going to therapy, journaling, being in nature, or calling someone to see how they're doing. *In what ways do you numb out? How could you check in instead?*

3. Nothing will kill your creativity more than the pressure to hurry, prove, or monetize. *How do you see this showing up in your days? Can you leave these things behind to create something beautiful?*

4. Space to be with God will be breeding grounds for growth. Get honest. Ask someone to hold up a mirror so you can better see yourself. *Are there struggles you need to bring into the light? Are there confessions you need to make? Is there anything you're trying to hide?*

5. Love your space and your rhythms, but love your people more. As you create and experience life with more space and better boundaries, it could be easy to be selfish. *What interruptions should always trump your rhythms?*

Schedule

To create new and sustainable rhythms of
work, play, and rest be sure you write out
your schedule hour by hour to analyze
where things are at and what needs to
change. You can't get where you want to go
until you know where you're at.

About The Author

Manda Carpenter married the guy she swore she'd never date, quit her job, sold her car, moved to Chicago, and became a foster mama. God's grace has literally wrecked her life in the very best way. She's a firm believer that there isn't a single person you would not love if you knew their story. A writer by day and an unashamed Oreo addict by night, Manda lives by the motto "Impressing is Exhausting" and started a movement, *Monthly Letters of Encouragement*, to help bring light and hope to people in dark situations. Her next book is releasing with Zondervan in early 2021.